CONQUERING WORRY

*How To Deal
With Stress In Your Life*

CONQUERING WORRY

*How To Deal
With Stress In Your Life*

BOB GASS
with Ruth Gass Halliday

TABLE OF CONTENTS

You're Doing It To Yourself! 9

Let Peace Rule 15

The "Top-Nine" Causes! 20

1 – Money 22

2 – Health 26

3 – Children 29

4 – The Demands Of Others 32

5 – Fear Of Failure 35

6 – Acceptance 38

7 – The Past 41

8 – The Future 44

9 – Death 47

What God Is Saying To You 49

Conquering Worry

All Scripture used in this book are King James Version unless otherwise indicated.

Scripture quotations marked AMP are taken from *The Amplified Bible, Old Testament*. Copyright © 1965, 1987 by the Zondervan Corporation. *The Amplified New Testament*, copyright © 1954, 1958, 1987 by the Lockman Foundation. Used by permission.

Scripture quotations marked CEV are taken from the *Contemporary English Version*, copyright © 1995, 1999 by American Bible Society, New York. Used by permission.

Scripture quotations marked NAS are from the *New American Standard Bible*. Copyright © 1960, 1962, 1963, 1968, 1971, 1972, 1975, 1977 by the Lockman Foundation. Used by permission.

Scripture quotations marked NCV are taken from *The Holy Bible, New Century Version*, copyright © 1987, 1988, 1991 by Word Publishing, Dallas, Texas 75234. Used by permission.

Scripture quotations marked NIV are taken from the *Holy Bible: New International Version*. Copyright © 1973, 1978, 1984 by the International Bible Society. Used by permission of Zondervan Bible Publishers.

Scripture quotations marked NLT are taken from the *Holy Bible, New Living Translation*, copyright © 1996. Used by permission of Tyndale House Publishers, Inc., Wheaton, Illinois 60189. All rights reserved.

Scripture quotations marked NKJV are taken from the *New King James Version*. Copyright ©1979, 1980, 1982, Thomas Nelson Inc., Publishers. Used by permission.

Scripture quotations marked TLB are from *The Living Bible*. Copyright © 1971 by Tyndale House Publishers, Wheaton, IL. Used by permission.

Scripture quotations marked TM are from *The Message: The New Testament, Psalms and Proverbs*. Copyright © 1993, 1994, 1995, 1996 by Eugene H. Peterson. Used by permission of NavPress Publishing Group.

CONQUERING WORRY: How To Deal With Stress In Your Life
Copyright ©2002 by Celebration Enterprises
P.O. Box 1045
Roswell, GA 30077-1045

ISBN 1-931727-97-X

SYNERGY PUBLISHERS
Gainesville, Florida 32635

Author's Photograph © Mary Robinette

Printed in the United States of America. All rights reserved. Under International Copyright Law, no part of this publication may be reproduced, stored, or transmitted by any means—electronic, mechanical, photographic (photocopy), recording, or otherwise—without written permission from the Publisher.

Notice to our American and Canadian readers: This book has been "Anglicized" for the British market, therefore certain words are spelled differently.

"Blessed (happy, fortunate, to be envied) is the man whom You discipline and instruct, O Lord, and teach out of Your law.

That You may give him power to keep himself calm

in the days of adversity."

Psalm 94:12-13 AMP

You're Doing It To Yourself!

Worry is something you *permit*. Peace is something you *pursue*!

Jesus said, "Stop allowing yourselves to be agitated and disturbed; do not permit yourselves to be fearful" (Jn 14:27 AMP).

That means you can *learn* to control what goes on in your mind!

How? By filling it with God's Word!

Not just the Word you read casually, but: (a) The Word you *process* mentally. (b) The Word you *apply* to each situation as it arises. (c) The Word you *stand* on in times of crisis, because you know it's your right to have the peace, the protection, and the provision God promises.

For years I tried to use my faith to remove anything that didn't *feel* good or that I didn't *like*. What frustration!

Finally I began to realise that what I needed to

do was use my faith to go calmly through the storm. I needed to stop allowing the enemy to steal my peace every time I turned around.

Jesus said, "Stop allowing yourselves to be agitated."

I was doing it to myself!

The only power stress and worry have over me, is the power I *give* them.

And it's the same with you!

Jesus rebuked His disciples because they lost their peace in the storm (Mk 4:40). He didn't lose His, He was asleep in the back of the boat. Where are *you* today? Resting with Jesus in the back of the boat, or panicking with the disciples in the front?

Stress and worry take over when you forget two things:

(1) *What God has told you!* Listen, "Let us go over to the other side" (Mk 4:35 NIV). Once Jesus had spoken those words there wasn't a wave big enough to take them under. Any time you are doing what God has told you to do, you *can't* go under – never forget that!

You're Doing It To Yourself!

(2) *Who is with you in the boat!* They thought they knew Jesus pretty well, but before the night was over they were asking "Who is this? Even the wind and the waves obey him!" (Mk 4:41 NIV).

The Lord has permitted the storm you're going through right now to show you that: (a) You don't have a problem He can't solve. (b) You may be powerless in the circumstances, but He's not. (c) You're not alone, He's with you. (d) Through this experience you'll come to know Him in a way you've never known Him before.

Stress is brought on by trying to do something, about something you can't do anything about. For example:

(1) *Trying to change the people in your life.* People can't change other people, only God can! And He does, when we back off, love them as they are (which doesn't mean we have to endorse everything they do), pray and speak God's Word over them, then allow Him to deal with it *His* way, in *His* time, and for *His* glory.

(2) *Trying to make things happen when the time's not*

right. Listen, "There is a time for everything, and a season for every activity under heaven" (Ecc 3:1 NIV). One of the characteristics of a child is *impatience*; they can't wait for anything. God wants you to outgrow childish impatience! He told Habakkuk, "The revelation awaits an appointed time...though it linger, wait for it; it will certainly come" (Hab 2:3 NIV).

(3) *Getting upset with yourself because you're not progressing fast enough.* You can slow down your growth by neglecting the spiritual disciplines of prayer and daily Bible reading, but ultimately *only God's Spirit* can change you and produce in you the characteristics of Christ. Paul writes, "But we all, with open face beholding as in a glass the glory of the Lord, are changed into the same image from glory to glory, [grade to grade]...*by the Spirit of the Lord*" (2 Cor 3:18). Trying to change yourself is like trying to pick yourself up by your own shoelaces, it can't be done! You never "arrive." From the new birth to the new Jerusalem – you're always a work in progress.

(4) *Pushing yourself harder and harder.* I know, I've done it. I was doing what *I* had determined to be

God's will in the matter, without actually seeking Him as to what *He* wanted me to do, *when* He wanted me to do it, and how *much*! And I wore myself and everybody else out in the process.

If you make your work more important than yourself, you won't be around to finish it! How is it that the mighty fall? Because they don't understand the importance of *balance* and *rest*.

Listen, "God ended His work…and He rested" (Gen 2:2 NKJV). Think about that! God did – but we don't! Why? Because:

We set goals without consulting Him! Jesus said, "My yoke is easy, and my burden is light" (Mt 11:30). When something is either too *hard* or too *heavy*, you can be sure God didn't give it to you.

We lose perspective! We tell ourselves, "I'm doing this for my family." Oh yeah? Has it occurred to you that given the choice, our families would rather have more of *us* and less of other things? But we don't give them that option, do we?

Personal empowerment begins when we take control of *what* happens in our lives, and *when* it happens.

Never feel guilty about taking a break – God did. Time taken to rest your body and replenish your soul is better than a trip aborted.

Let Peace Rule!

Paul wrote, "Let the peace (soul harmony which comes) from Christ rule (act as umpire continually) in your hearts [deciding and settling with finality all questions that arise in your minds]" (Col 3:15 AMP).

Let peace rule! Make that your motto!

The first thing you lose when you step out of God's will is your peace. So if you don't have peace, don't proceed! Listen, "Ye shall go out with joy, and be led forth with *peace*" (Isa 55:12).

Many times peace is *all* God will give you to let you know whether you're – in or out – of His will.

Every time I've violated "the peace rule" I've regretted it, because it's a lot easier to get into things than it is to get out of them.

When all hell is breaking loose around you, yet you can remain calm and confident, you're experiencing, "The peace of God, which transcends all understanding" (Phil 4:7 NIV).

How do you get this peace?

Listen, "Don't worry about anything; instead, pray about everything; tell God your needs and don't forget to thank him for his answers. If you do this you will experience God's peace, which is far more wonderful than the human mind can understand. His peace will keep your thoughts and your hearts quiet and at rest" (Phil 4:6-7 TLB).

Notice the words "Don't worry about anything; instead, pray about everything."

The prayer of commitment moves the burden from you to Jesus!

Peter writes, "Let him have all your worries and cares, for he is always thinking about you and watching everything that concerns you. Be careful – watch out for attacks from Satan…He prowls around like a hungry, roaring lion, looking for some victim to tear apart. Stand firm when he attacks. Trust the Lord; and remember that other Christians… are going through these sufferings too. After you have suffered a little while, our God, who is full of kindness…will…personally…come and pick you up, and set you firmly in place, and make you

Let Peace Rule

stronger than ever (1 Pet 5:7-10 TLB).

Don't give the devil a few days to work you over! The longer you wait to resist him the stronger his hold over you will become.

The moment you begin to worry, stop and ask yourself, *"What's the enemy trying to do here? If I give in to these negative emotions what will the end result be?"*

Paul writes, "Do not give the devil a foothold" (Eph 4:27 NIV). He also writes, "Don't let him outwit you" (See 2 Cor 2:11 NIV). Learn to be smarter than your enemy! Even though Satan has studied you for years and knows your areas of weakness, you can put him to flight every time by standing on God's Word and declaring, "It is written."

How well do you know God's Word? When problems arise do you find yourself wishing you knew more of it?

The new birth brings a new battle; if you're going to win it you must know how to use the sword of the Scriptures. Listen, "Finally, be strong in the Lord and in his [not your] mighty power. Put on the full armour of God so that you can take your

Conquering Worry

stand against the devil's schemes...take...*the sword of the Spirit, which is the word of God*" (See Eph 6:10-17 NIV).

The sword referred to here was a large dagger used by Roman soldiers to fight at close range.

Understand this clearly: you'll have to stand toe-to-toe with your enemy! To defeat him you'll need to know how to use the Word of God, because it's, "Living...Sharper than any double-edged sword, it penetrates...it judges the thoughts and attitudes of the heart" (Heb 4:12 NIV).

God's Word can determine with pinpoint accuracy exactly what's going on in your life. When you come face to face with the enemy, it's the only weapon capable of rendering him powerless.

But to use it you must first *know* it! It must become your automatic response to every challenge.

If a situation calls for *thanksgiving*, then a word of praise should come alive in your mind and flow from your lips.

If a situation demands *confrontation*, a word of rebuke, deliverance, and counsel should come alive in your mind and flow from your lips.

If a situation is rooted in *lies*, a word of truth should come alive in your mind and flow from your lips.

If you really want to *hurt* the enemy where it counts, start declaring The Word of God to him and he'll flee.

He has to!

He can't handle being repeatedly stabbed and slashed by the sword of God's Word, *which is the very life of God.*

The "Top Nine" Causes!

Surveys consistently show that the top nine things we worry about are: (1) Money. (2) Health. (3) Children. (4) The demands of others. (5) The fear of failure. (6) Acceptance. (7) The past. (8) The future. (9) Death.

Let's look at each, and see what God has to say. After all, when you get *His* opinion what difference does anybody else's make?

Worry is an inside job – so is conquering it. Furthermore, most of the things we worry over are things we can do little or nothing about.

"How can I change that?" you ask.

By focusing on the things you can do something about, like your *perspective* and your *attitude*. Isaiah writes, "Thou wilt keep him in perfect peace whose mind is stayed (focused) on thee: because he trusteth in thee" (Isa 26:3).

Worry reveals a lack of confidence in God. Either

The "Top Nine" Causes!

you haven't turned the situation over to Him, or you've taken it back because He didn't handle it the *way* you thought He would, or within the *time* you thought He should.

So, what do *you* worry about?

1 – MONEY

Do you worry about making ends meet? Putting your kids through college? Having enough for retirement?

David said, "I have been young, and now I am old; yet have I not seen the righteous forsaken, [I bet you haven't either] nor his seed begging bread" (Ps 37:25).

God promised His people, "Even to your old age…I am he who will sustain you. I have made you and I will carry you" (Isa 46:4 NIV).

Jesus said, "Don't worry at all about having enough food and clothing…your heavenly Father already knows perfectly well that you need them, and he will give them to you if you give him first place in your life and live as he wants you to. So don't be anxious about tomorrow. God will take care of your tomorrow too. Live one day at a time" (Matt 6:31-34 TLB).

Each morning when the Children of Israel wakened up there was enough manna for that day,

1 – Money

waiting at the door of their tent. Each day they got up counting on God's faithfulness, and in forty years He never missed a day.

And their God is your God!

Jesus told us to pray, "Give us this day our *daily* bread" (Matt 6:11), because He wants us to live in *the moment*; in day-tight-compartments. He won't give you tomorrow's answers or tomorrow's grace, so don't waste your time asking for them. His Word to you is "live one day at a time."

When it comes to money keep three things in mind:

(1) *God owns everything!* Your name may be on the deed, but don't get any wrong ideas. Listen: "*All* things come from You, and out of Your own [hand] we have given You" (1 Chron 29:14 AMP). You're just the administrator of His estate and the executor of His will, so when He tells you to give a certain amount, don't say, "I'll think about it." And don't try to bargain; for on the other end of every act of obedience, there is a blessing waiting. God said, "Oh, that their hearts would be inclined to…keep all

my commands always, *so that it might go well* with them" (Deut 5:29 NIV). Want things to go well for you? Do what God tells you – it's that simple!

(2) *God alone is your source!* You don't have a thing He didn't give you. Without Him you couldn't even catch your next breath! It's okay to enjoy your money, to invest and share it, as long as you don't *trust* in it. The Bible says we're to trust only in God, "Who giveth us richly all things to enjoy" (1 Tim 6:17).

(3) *Every spending decision is a spiritual decision!* Your cheque book will always reflect your values, goals, and priorities. What does *yours* say? When it came to giving, the Macedonian Christians were a class act. Listen, "They gave not only what they could afford, but far more…their first action was to dedicate themselves to the Lord and…*whatever directions God might give to them through us*" (2 Cor 8:3-5 TLB). When God has access to your heart, He'll have access to your finances too!

True financial freedom comes when giving no longer threatens your sense of security, because you know – you absolutely know – that God is the supplier of your every need, and that consecutive sowing *guarantees* consecutive reaping. (See 2 Cor 9:6).

What a way to live!

2 – HEALTH

Do you worry about your health? Do you fear cancer? Or heart disease? Or diabetes? Do certain sicknesses seem to run in your family? Worrying can actually wear down your immune system and make you vulnerable to the very things you fear.

Facts are different from truth!

It may be a *fact* that certain sicknesses run in your family, but the *truth* is you don't have to get them, because God promises in His word, "I will take away sickness from among you, and…give you a full life span" (Ex 23:25-26 NIV). His Word to you is: "Pay attention to what I say; listen closely to my words…for they are life to those who find them and *health* to [your] whole body" (Prov 4:20-22 NIV).

Does that mean we can eat anything we want and live as we please? No, we have a part to play in maintaining good health!

The *NEWSTART* programme in California offers

2 – Health

a simple, easy-to-remember acronym for enjoying good health.

N – *nutrition*. Are you eating properly? If not, it will affect your health, your energy levels, and your moods.

E – *exercise*. God didn't create our bodies to be sedentary. Walking, even a mile a day, (twenty minutes on your treadmill) will dramatically improve your health.

W – *water*. Are your drinking enough? (Six to eight glasses a day). If not, your immune system becomes weak, your kidneys can't flush out impurities, and you set the stage for sickness.

S – *sunlight*. Light triggers two hormones responsible for preventing the blues. The "feel good" seratonin, and the "good sleep" melatonin. That's why some people get depressed when the days are shorter and darker.

T – *temperance*. Are you out of control in certain areas? It's essential that you submit your thoughts, your will, your emotions, and your appetites to God – daily.

A – *air*. Are you getting enough fresh air?

Inhaling deeply? Fully expanding your lungs?

R – *rest*. You need a good eight hours to complete the three cycles of sleep necessary to rejuvenate your body, otherwise you're not at your best.

T – *trust in God*. Trust is the highest form of faith because it doesn't need to know all the answers. It simply believes that, "Everything is working for my good and God's glory." (See Rom 8:28).

Make up your mind today to get in shape, for while *God's* responsible for your healing, *you're* responsible for maintaining your health!

3 – CHILDREN

Do you worry about your children? Getting into bad company? Involved in drugs or alcohol? Becoming the victim of a pornographer or a pedophile on the Internet? Succumbing to Aids or pre-marital pregnancy? Do you struggle with guilt because your job takes you away from them for so much of the time?

God's promise to you is, "Your children will have God for their teacher – what a mentor" (Isa 54:13 TM).

In the early 1800's the Swiss educator, Johann Pestalozzi, wrote, "The best way for a child to learn about God, is to know a real Christian. The best way for them to discover the power of prayer, is to live with parents who pray." Right on!

Eighty-five-percent of all children raised this way develop a strong personal faith – before age thirteen.

"Am I responsible for my child's spiritual choices?" Ultimately, no. Potentially, yes. If you want to take the spiritual temperature of any family, put a

thermometer in the mouths of the parents.

"But my kids are already grown? Isn't it too late?" No, God's name is "Redeemer" – He can give you another chance. Repent and commit your life to Christ. That's how generational cycles of failure are broken, and God is brought back into the picture.

"But what if I'm concerned about bringing a child into an evil world?" That's the whole point; it's children of the light who push back the darkness. Instead of reacting out of fear, selfishness, or convenience, use your family to impact the world for God.

"But how can I compete with the negative influences around me?" Every study confirms that a parent has by far the greatest influence – greater than friends, school, or the media – in determining the character and direction of a child.

The prophet Malachi wrote, "Did He not make them one?…and why one? He seeks godly offspring" (Mal 2:15 NJKV). In God's mind marriage is the *starting point* for populating the world with people who will serve Him.

Think: that tiny creature who sleeps when you're awake, is wide awake when you're asleep, has

3 – Children

a set of lungs that could drown out *The Concorde*, whose face you could forget because you spend so much time at the other end – is your greatest mission field.

Think of it as a relay race!

Success isn't based on how well you run as an individual, but on how well you pass the baton.

Only when the story of future generations is told will you know if you won or lost. David says, "You have taught me from my youth…Now also when I am old…do not forsake me, until I declare Your strength to this generation, Your power to everyone who is to come" (Ps 71:17-18 NKJV).

Don't drop the baton! Make your goal to raise children who'll pick up your legacy of faith and take it *further* than you ever did.

When you do that, God will work with you! Listen, "Believe on the Lord Jesus Christ, and thou shalt be saved, and *thy house*" (Acts 16:31). And again, "The promise is unto you, *and to your children*" (Acts 2:39).

Pray and claim your children for God – for heaven responds when godly parents pray.

4 – THE DEMANDS OF OTHERS

Are you a people pleaser? Is your self-worth based on the approval of your family, friends, and loved ones? If so you'll always live under stress. Why? Because when others give you self worth, they can also take it from you.

Paul wrote, "We make it our goal to please him [God]" (2 Cor 5:9 NIV).

Become a God-pleaser not a people-pleaser!

Ever notice that before an airliner takes off the attendants tell you that if the plane gets into trouble, to secure your *own* oxygen mask before attempting to help others with theirs? That's not selfish – it's smart! Unless you get enough oxygen how can you help anybody else?

Are *your* spiritual and emotional needs being met? Really? If not, it's time to stop taking care of everybody else and start learning to take care of yourself, before you burn out.

4 – The Demands Of Others

You can't travel quietly through life hoping *others* will see when your "cup is full." *Speak up*, or they'll just keep pouring on more problems and more responsibilities!

You don't have to drop a bomb or start a riot, but you do need to learn when to say "enough!" Your life is too precious to leave in somebody else's hands, especially if they're needy, demanding, or just plain manipulative.

If you want to be heard, speak up!

Personal empowerment begins when you take control of your life.

Overloaded people fail; they always have and they always will. They fail at marriage, ministry, and management. They fail at parenting, partnership, and professional endeavors.

You're like an airplane; if you carry too much baggage you won't get off the ground. Motivated by a desire to please or impress, you'll take on too much, and in the end, fail to reach the heights God planned for you, or crash because you ignored your limitations!

Every situation that arises does not warrant your

attention! Think about that!

Jesus left the crowd to be alone with the Father. Did He evoke criticism from the crowd? Yes! Did He enjoy communion with God? Yes!

And you'll have to make that same choice too.

People who don't recognise your needs and respect your goals will drain you, divert you, and keep you grounded.

What's the answer?

Give what you can, learn when to say "enough," then let go and fly!

5 – Fear Of Failure

Opportunities are coming toward you every day – or passing you by.

There are no risk-free success stories. The road to success is through multiple failures. Always!

Ask any experienced trapeze artist. He'll tell you that to be good at it you must learn to do four things: (a) Launch out. (b) Let go. (c) Hold still. (d) Expect to be caught.

And it takes practice – lots of it – including falling into the safety net more times than you can count.

What stage are you at?

Stage 1: Launch out! You can't walk on water if you're not willing to get out of the boat. Faith means walking to the very edge, stepping into the unknown, confident that when you do, God will either put solid rock under your feet – or teach you to fly!

Stage 2: Let go! "Let go of what?" you ask. Your need to control either the method or the outcome. Your desire to look good or get the credit. Your stubborn ways. Your independent streak.

Stage 3: Hold still! When people say, "Don't just stand there, do something," but God says, "Don't just do something, stand there," you've a decision to make. You're in a 'Red Sea' situation. God has spoken to you, but not a soul around would believe you if you shared it. So what do you do? "Stand firm and you will see the deliverance of the Lord" (See Ex 14:13 NIV). Obey God! Let Him vindicate you!

Stage 4: Expect to be caught! That's what Jack Hayford meant when he wrote the chorus, "I anticipate the inevitable, supernatural, intervention of God, I expect a miracle." What are you anticipating? David anticipated only the best, listen: "My hope comes from him…I shall not be shaken" (Ps 62:5-6 NIV).

God's word to you today is – Launch out! Let go! Hold still! Expect to be caught!

5 – Fear of Failure

Do you need more wisdom?

The Bible says, "The Lord confides in those who fear him" (Ps 25:14 NIV).

"Would God reveal His will to somebody like me?"

Yes! Listen: "The Sovereign Lord does nothing without revealing his plan to his servants" (Amos 3:7 NIV). Listen again: "Everything that I learned from my Father I have made known to you" (Jn 15:15 NIV). And again: "Your ears will hear a voice behind you, saying, 'This is the way; walk ye in it'" (Isa 30:21).

What more do you need?

6 – ACCEPTANCE

Do *you feel like you don't measure up?* In terms of looks? Education? Social status? Are you constantly wishing you were somebody else? If so, listen:

"So, what do you think? With God on our side like this, how can we lose? If God didn't hesitate to put everything on the line for us…is there anything else he wouldn't gladly and freely do for us? And who would dare tangle with God by messing with one of God's chosen? Who would dare even to point a finger? The One who died for us – who was raised to life for us! – is in the presence of God at this very moment sticking up for us. Do you think anyone is going to be able to drive a wedge between us and Christ's love for us? There is no way! Not trouble, not hard times, not hatred, not hunger, not homelessness, not bullying threats, not backstabbing, not even the worst sins listed in Scripture…None of this fazes us because Jesus loves us. I'm absolutely

6 – Acceptance

convinced that nothing – nothing living or dead, angelic or demonic, today or tomorrow, high or low, thinkable or unthinkable – absolutely *nothing* can get between us and God's love" (Rom 8:31-39 TM).

Imagine being loved like that by – *God!* What status! What pedigree! What assurance!

No matter how unworthy you may feel today, you cannot shut off, or in any way diminish the flow of God's love towards you.

Nothing can change the way He feels about you. *Nothing* can alter the fact that He's going to continue to love you no matter what you do or say. *Never* lose sight of that, because God's love will heal your emotions, raise your low self-esteem, and put a foundation of worth and dignity under you. It's what allows you to respect yourself!

It'll also motivate you to discipline yourself, because when you truly value something, you want to *protect* it and *develop* it to the max!

God's love gives you the capacity to love yourself, then love others. When you can do that the circle is complete.

Just think, you're not only chosen by God,

you're eternally, passionately, tenderly and unconditionally loved by Him. There's no greater blessing, no greater assurance than that.

Stop despising the qualities that make you unique!

You were born at just the right time, in just the right place, and with just the right gifts to fulfill a plan that *nobody* but you can fulfil.

Open your Bible and see what God thinks of you.

David the Psalmist wrote, "You saw me before I was born and scheduled each day of my life before I began to breathe. Every day was recorded in your Book! How precious it is, Lord, to realise that you are thinking about me constantly!" (Ps 139:16-17 TLB).

God's opinion of you, and that alone, is the only reliable basis on which to build your self worth. Never forget that!

7 – THE PAST

Do you worry about your past? Do you stress-out over situations you can't change? Do yesterday's failures prey on your mind, filling you with guilt and condemnation? If so, listen to what God says:

"Their sins…will I remember no more" (Heb 8:12).

God didn't say that because He's forgetful, He said it because He *chooses* not to remember your sins.

When *you* choose otherwise, you: (a) question the quality of His forgiveness; (b) declare your standards to be higher than His; (c) allow the enemy to bring you into condemnation; (d) forfeit the confidence you need to pray for and receive what He has for you.

When you rehearse your past failures you not only keep them alive, you *empower* them. What you keep on deposit you're more likely to withdraw and act on in the hour of weakness.

Just as nobody can predict when a dormant volcano will erupt, you can't predict when an unresolved issue will resurface and come roaring out of your subconscious, turning your words into hot coals, and your behaviour into a blaze of destruction.

Only by forgiving yourself – and others – can you truly break the hold the past has over you, and get on with your life.

Shame is not a blessing; it's a weight that Jesus carried for you on the cross. Set it down and walk away! You have the right to do that because His word says, "As far as the east is from the west, so far hath he removed our transgressions from us" (Ps 103:12).

Anytime Satan brings up your past, it's because: (a) he's running low on material; (b) he hopes you are ignorant of the truth; (c) he fears your future.

You ask, "What should I do?" Just point him to the cross, refuse to discuss it further, and keep moving forward!

In spite of the fact that Joseph was betrayed by his brothers and slandered by Potiphar's wife, he could say, "You meant evil against me; but God

7 – The Past

meant it for good" (Gen 50:20 NKJV).

How often has something happened in your life that you later realised was necessary? If you hadn't sustained *this*, or walked through *that*, you wouldn't be ready for the blessings you're enjoying *now*, right?

It's when you see the hand of God at work in it, that you begin to understand that what the enemy intended for your destruction, God used for your development.

To be more than a conqueror means to stand up and say, *"Here's how I see it. It took everything I've been through to make me who I am today, and to teach me what I know. I choose to be better, not bitter. I trust the faithfulness of God more than ever. If faith doesn't move the mountain, it will give me strength to endure until tomorrow. And if it's not gone by tomorrow, I'll still believe that God is able and trust Him until He does."*

Rejoice! Your steps (and your stops) are being arranged by God (See Ps 37:23). They're also being observed by Him. When you get through this, you'll realise that "the worst thing that could have happened" was, in reality, "the Lord's doing," and it'll become "marvellous in your eyes" (See Matt 21:42).

8 – THE FUTURE

Do *you worry about what the future holds?* Then listen, "Like an open book…all the stages of my life were spread out before you" (Ps 139:16 TM).

God's plan for you was already in place before you were born. His blueprint included *every* detail from start to finish! Your only obligation is to choose what He's *already* chosen for you, to say "yes" to what He's already designed for you.

Paul writes, "You'll do best by…meditating on…the best, not the worst" (Phil 4:8 TM).

Are you blessing-conscious or problem-conscious? Before you answer, consider this humorous story about identical twins: one an optimist, whose motto was "Everything's comin' up roses," and the other a pessimist, who always expected the worst. Their parents took them to a psychologist hoping to "balance out" their personalities. He suggested that on their next birthday they put each one in a

8 – The Future

separate room to open his gifts. "Give the pessimist the best toys you can afford," the therapist said, "and give the optimist a box of manure." Even though they were a bit shocked by his suggestions, they did what he asked.

First they peeped in at the pessimist and heard him complaining, "I don't like the colour of that toy. I don't want to play this game." Next they looked in on the optimist and saw him smiling, throwing manure up in the air and shouting, "You can't fool me. With this much manure, there's gotta be a pony!"

Whatever you look for you'll eventually find – whether good or bad!

If you're walking with God here's what you *should* be looking for.

Listen, "You will be blessed…wherever you go, both in coming and in going…your enemies…will attack you from one direction, but they will scatter from you in seven! The Lord will bless everything you do…the world will see that you are a people claimed by the Lord, and they will stand in awe of you. The Lord will give you an abundance of good things…the Lord will make you the head and not the tail, and you will always have the upper hand" (Deut 28:3-13 NLT).

Today, start *looking* for God's blessings!

9 – DEATH

Woody Allen once quipped, *"I don't mind dying, I just don't want to be there when it happens."* A lot of us feel that way.

But death is not the end – it's just the beginning of a life which will have no end.

When David thought about dying he wrote, "As for me, I will behold thy face in righteousness: I shall be satisfied when I awake with thy likeness" (Ps 17:15).

Imagine falling asleep, then wakening up – looking like Jesus!

Paul the Apostle said, "We can tell you with complete confidence…that when the Master comes again to get us, those of us who are still alive will not get a jump on the dead or leave them behind. In actual fact, they'll be ahead of us. The Master himself will…come down from heaven and the dead in Christ will rise – they'll go first…the rest of us…will be caught up with them…to meet the Master…then there will be *one huge family reunion*" (1Thess 4:15-17 TM).

How can I be sure? Because at the cross a showdown took place. Jesus called Satan's hand. Tired of seeing us intimidated, He went into the tomb called death, transformed it into a lighted underpass to heaven, came out triumphantly, and announced, "Death, who's afraid of you now?" (1 Cor 15:54 TM).

The Bible says, "By embracing death...he destroyed the Devil's hold on death and freed all who cower through life, scared to death of death" (Heb 2:14-15 TM).

At Dan Richardson's memorial service these written words were distributed: *Cancer is limited: it cannot cripple love, or corrode faith, or eat away peace, or destroy confidence, or kill friendship, or shut out memories, or silence courage, or invade the soul, or reduce eternal life, or lessen the power of the resurrection.*

Be encouraged today, God's planning *"a huge family reunion!"*

What God Is Saying To You

Some things God will do for us, other things He expects us to do for ourselves.

That's why the Bible says, "Blessed [happy, fortunate, to be envied] is the man whom you discipline and instruct, O Lord, and teach out of Your law...*you...give him power to keep himself calm in the days of adversity*" (Ps 94:12-13 AMP).

Want to be able to stay calm, regardless of the circumstances?

If so, God is saying to you:

"Live by My Word in *every* area of your life. Learn to be sensitive to my voice; quick to respond and to obey.

"My yoke is easy and My burden is light. I'll never give you anything too hard to handle or to heavy to carry.

"Give me each of your concerns – one by one as they arise. Delight yourself in My love, My provision, My protection, and I'll give you the desires of your heart.

"Because the devil is 'the accuser' he'll constantly point to your flaws and failures and tell you you're not worthy of My blessings. Don't listen to him – he's the father of lies!

"I've saved you by My grace and positioned you in Christ. I see you through the blood, therefore you are *always* worthy and acceptable before Me!

"Starting today, give Me all your anxieties and cares. Begin to live in the present, not the future. Look for My blessings and you'll find them. Enjoy life in all its fullness."

What's your habit?

We all struggle with habits – what's yours? Be honest!

Does the thought or suggestion of it become so strong within you that **you can't say "no?"** That habit has become a "stronghold."

But there's good news! We have power to demolish strongholds.

If you're ready to quit – *really* ready, this book will show you how!

Breaking Habits
Learning to Live in Freedom
A new book by Bob Gass

Call or write for your copy today.

Telephone 1-800-964-9846 or 1-678-461-9989
P.O. Box 767550, Roswell, GA 30076 U.S.A.
www.wordforyou.com

A New Book *by Bob Gass*

The six qualities of a winner – do you have them?

God said, "Because Caleb has a different spirit, I will bring him into the Promised Land."

Winners don't necessarily have more education or fewer problems, they just have "a different spirit."

Read this book and discover the **"6 principles"** every winner lives by!

The Winning Life
How to Succeed at Anything

To order, call: 1-800-964-9846
or 1-678-461-9989

Visit our website at: ***www.wordforyou.com***

AUTHOR'S PHOTOGRAPH ©MARY ROBINETTE

New Insights On *Marriage*
From Bob Gass

Are you happy with your marriage?
Would you like it to be better?

The keys are ... *commitment* ... *communication* ... *compromise*. And you can learn to use them.

If you want to **"spice up"** a dull marriage, **"shore up"** a shaky one, or take yours and **"make it better"** – this book's for you.

A BETTER MARRIAGE: *Keys to Intimacy and Growth*

Order your copy today. 1-800-964-9846 or 1-678-461-9989